as
time
passes

brenden daniel

ISBN-13: 978-1542811194
ISBN-10: 1542811198

for people like me

but mostly
for those we've hurt

as
time
passes

before we start

so it was a breakup. not an especially rough one, nothing
tumultuous or angry. but an especially hard one, for me
at least. hard like i didn't know it would be. like i didn't
know it could be. though in one minor sense i was glad
to be able to verify in that moment that i could feel
something strong- anything- with that much passion.

i had started to suspect this new depth of emotion some
time before, and had it certified once already in the most
beautiful of ways- when i first knew i could love. but i
was too late. too late when all the while i unknowingly
gave an ever-swelling heartache to a girl who trusted me
with her heart from the beginning.

though losing her to that heartache did confirm that i
could even experience the full spectrum of emotions. all
the highs and all the lows were within my range, albeit far
from under my control. and having then become
acquainted with those absolute lows, i wanted nothing
more than to instantly take it all back. to leave that packet
of wonder for a discovery date of never and continue on
in my ignorance.

but that's not what happened, not at all. because it hurt
awfully bad to have to recover from falling off those highs.

because i had a lot to learn along the way to become someone worthy of a fraction of what i'd lost in her. and that's what my story is about.

though this girl i hurt so deeply, she was far and away the most amazing person in my life. nothing but loving and caring, and unfortunately, she was too accepting for too long. so long that the damage i did by not properly returning that love, broke something deep within her. so her experience is here all throughout as well, from her most personal space- the pages of her journal.

we're ultimately two people traveling two different paths to try and feel whole. one i see as victim, purely. the other i hope can be viewed with compassion because, well, it's me. because i'm trying and finally putting in the work i wish more than anything i had done before it were too late- before i ever let down this special girl like i did.

but now, here we are instead. let's begin.

it's still true...

I

if you're looking, you can find her-
she's as sweet and nice as ever.
she carries it well, her silent reminder,
she laughs and is just as clever.

though if one had known her before all this,
could they say she's just the same?
as if all those cardiac nicks and pricks
don't amount to lasting pain.

now time has a way of healing the damage
while leaving some bumps behind.
when sometimes it's more than a young girl can manage,
she finds herself slowly resigned.

so when he finally discovered
his heart was uncovered,
he said it proud but he said it too late.
when he told her at last he certainly loved her,
she could no longer relate.

her kiss
she could sedate and excite me
all in one breath,
stop my heart and quicken it-

she could have loved me to death.

entry 1

i love him now
in this moment
i do

but i need him
to earn my future
to make me believe
in a vision of us
beyond now

because this moment
cannot last
forever

telescope
we drove out to the edge of town
and stopped in an abandoned lot.
i took her hand and led her down
to where i'd found the perfect spot.

far away from all the cars
and the harshest city light,
where we had a view of all the stars
on a moonless, cloudless night.

we went by foot down a long dirt road
where trespassing is forbidden,
through a field of grass that's pretty remote
and to the telescope i'd hidden.

the joy that spread across her face
was something better than surprise.
i had no need to gaze in space
when i could look into her eyes.

beneath starlight, on top of grass,
i laid our picnic meant for two.
we poured merlot, i had one more glass
and planned what i was about to do.

to finally make up for our past
and put her anxious mind to rest,
just that time had come at last
when i was ready to confess.

as she had done some time before,
yet still, i was overdue.
she was the only girl that i adored
but she had to know i loved her too.

i'm not just the boy who shows you the stars,
let's set out for the stars together.
i love you and everything that you are,
i want me and you forever.

these are the words i had in my head
and the truth is, i really meant it.
these are the words i wish i had said,
that some part of my mind prevented.

because another truth is i was scared,
just terrified i wasn't worthy.
not to say i didn't care,
but sure i'd fail her on this journey.

i knew she was perfect, better even,
and i knew she deserved far more.
i didn't want to be misleading
so i had to be better than before.

i wasn't certain the timing's right,
i wasn't yet who i ought to be.
so rather than tell her on this night,
i tried to act responsibly.

just then she looked to me and smiled
that most stunning smile i'd ever know.
which i haven't seen in quite a while,
it seems her smile was the first to go.

because the words i said instead
left a gap as big as a lie.
i know now she did feel misled
and she couldn't figure why.

it didn't matter that she heard it
a few months later on.
this was the night that she deserved it
and i couldn't say she's wrong.
she loved me. i did not return it-

and now it's gone.

entry 2

you always know
just the right way to act
just the right words to say
to keep me still with you
but you keep me
at a distance
so i know who you are
but i don't yet know
you like i need to

i think *let me inside*
let me explore your soul
find undiscovered treasures
unseen wonders
let me explore like
you explore my body

and then i think
but my soul too is unexplored
why do you only penetrate
my body

when the temple of who i am
that contains who i can be
is undisturbed

entry 3

happy and confused
sad and a little anxious
angry and excited

hopeful but not for long

these are all
the things i feel
and you are most
of the reasons why

no worries
in the heat of a summer solstice,
worries melt away to a new verse one.
laughter is louder and more frequent too-

in the midst of summer's first sun.

entry 4

it works
at the extremes
it's unbearable
in moderation

like coffee
steaming hot
ice cold
i can't do in between

i cannot have him
in between

keep this moment
if i could just keep this moment here,
this very one we're in-
i would hope it lasts at least a year,
and all the good within.

i wonder, is that not still too brief?
or else, in fact, too great?
i have always been of the belief
one should not question fate.

but now i've found my favorite moment,
a thought that comes to mind-
i think i'd rather like to own it,
to be forever mine.

though from all i know of moments past,
they only come and go.
there is no sure way to make it last,
nor one to make it slow.

if now behaves like moments i've met
and time won't break its stride,
i'll have to take some care to not let
this moment pass me by.

i'll remember all the sights and sounds
and how it made me feel,
as my moment now is winding down,
ignoring my appeal.

it's not one i'll be allowed to keep-
it's quicker than it seems.
so when i next lay my head to sleep,
i'll see it in my dreams.

though perhaps we are best off this way,
that just may be the case.
if i had this moment every day,
what good is heaven's grace?

entry 5

the promise of night
is a mind
free to wander
with no worries
until dawn

but lately
that luxury has been
held captive by thoughts of us

the kind that keep me up
precisely because
i don't think
they do the same to you

entry **6**

i can't really
blame him
that's who he is
that's what he offers
he told me so soon enough

so what am i doing
trying to change him

i can't be a lighthouse
when i have places
to go

standing still to guide him
when i need too
need to move
need to grow

i'm not just here
to light his path

i cannot
stand still

uncertain certainty
i'd been suspecting for a while,
but still it caught me unawares.
i blame that precious, peculiar smile
that flipped my heart in a kiss we shared.

it's that way you grin after such a kiss-
it affects me strangely, i can't deny.
when in your gaze, i found my bliss
and drowned my attention in your eyes.

in that moment, i could confirm
i had something else to guide my mind-
logic was gone and would not return
as emotion surged every nerve inside.

i don't quite know how or really when,
just that i first knew it then.

it fast became this most certain thing,
one of most uncertain origin.
the one thing certain that i knew-

i'm certainly in love with you.

entry 7

he finally said it
but i don't think
i feel it

what should
loved
feel like

i look down and see
my feet are firmly planted
no risk of floating
off on a cloud
i look up and see
no rose tint
if anything the world seems
a little more blue

i look at him
i can almost see
through him

entry 8

blue is almost the right word
the right slice of the spectrum
at least

i think of all the shades
of blue i know

baby
sky
powder
royal
bice
navy
cerulean
midnight

it's none of these
but there are plenty more

i'll know them soon
i'm sure

past due

i think misfortune's coming soon,
though i really could not say.
but i suspect i am a bit past due
for something awful on this day.

so far it's been nothing of note,
nor superb in any fashion.
although if my luck has the only vote,
something lousy is bound to happen.

now if i may intervene a tad
to speak a word on my behalf-
i propose we do postpone the bad
that i'm for sure about to have.

i know it will find me in due time,
with so much hanging by a thread.
but for now i'm doing kind of fine,
i would prefer tomorrow instead.

or once everything's already wrong
and nothing's going my way.
that's when i say to pile it on,
but please don't harm today.

entry **9**

not just tired of waiting
i was broken from waiting
my shoulder burdened
my eyes weary
my touch cool

all the signs
of human atrophy
and you remained idle
you didn't act to save us

there are other ways too
so many ways i am human

when without proper love
we break

and break up

ball of confusion
how could you do this to me, to us?
you know i love you, now why can't we discuss
why you're walking away, without hesitation?
with no how come and no explanation.
why are you doing this, leaving me stranded?
you shut me out and i cannot understand it.
i'm so confused, is there more that you wanted?
or was this all something twisted you plotted?
did i even know you, was this all a game?
do you get any pleasure from giving me pain?
i told you before that we shouldn't do this.
i couldn't love at all and you even knew this.
but you stayed and made sure that you had me,
and you finally did, i loved you so madly.
before you took my heart and threw it in dirt-

i couldn't love, but also couldn't get hurt.

II

yes, he sure took a while to show it,
but still he knew he loved her, yet.
he'll never see more gorgeous eyes
and now he's walked the miles to know it.
in his mind as bold, lined, italicized-
hers is a smile he'd never forget.

so you could say she's plain in style,
mild in demeanor.
some may pass her on the avenue
and swear they'd never seen her.
but for him- for one more chance to see that smile,
he took the only path he knew,
hoping that if he wandered for long
he would find her wandering too.

and over the years he traveled along
that same road quite a bit,
'til he heard an almost familiar song.
if he strained some- yes, it just might fit!
it's the same one she would often hum,
now just the notes were kind of altered-
the melody subdued.
twice he thought her pitch had faltered,
but his fingers nearly began to drum,
so it was close enough to true.

entry 10

leaving him
isn't effortless
it's taken all of me

though may not seem it
when there's hardly
anything left
to take

entry *11*

i left it out there
probably for too long
exposed to the elements

that wasn't wise
allowing it to get this cold

so now it's a little
worse for wear
and heavy too
bogged down from
those cloudy rainy days

did someone step on it
because this seems more
than incidental contact
these cuts and bruises
this particular damage
with an imprint
of serial disregard

yes it was definitely
open and vulnerable
for too long

i thought perhaps
you'd notice it
and you'd take it in
to keep it safe for me
i was hoping that you
could be its warm place

probably wasn't smart but
it's easier to know that now
easier to make decisions now

now that my heart
is too broken to weigh in

tomorrow today
tomorrow, what a pleasant notion.
that of a brand new day.
now i wonder if it would cause a commotion,
yes, i wonder if i may
perhaps, by chance, go forth and borrow
a bit of tomorrow today.

because i might have messed this one up a tad.
i think, though i'm not quite sure.
i tried reshaping and smoothing it over,
tried with everything i had.
but it only got worse as the day grew older
and i can't seem to find the right cure.

though if i go get my tools and a bit of tomorrow,
i can maybe patch this one up-
a piece of sunrise in a clear blue sky
and i'll be careful to match it enough.
i can make it look decent, not really a lie
if no one asks how i got through today.
i'll put it together so nobody will know
and if i'm lucky i won't have to say.

but it may take a bit more of tomorrow,
so i can really do this thing right.

i'll see that promise covers all sorrow,
paste morning dew right over the rain,
and that should take it through to night.
now fresh lemonade to replace any pain,
on top of crying, put children at play-

oh, how i so do wish i could borrow
a bit of tomorrow today.

entry 12

he's the one
who made whole galaxies
full of wonder
seem so near

who i once thought
might pluck a star
just for me

he's the one
who then showed me
how far away they really are

the stars
in the galaxies
we will never reach

entry 13

when you refused
to be tied down
i tried to tie
myself to you

and was happy
to soar away
with you
until i dropped
hard

i guess those ties
weren't quite
secure enough

or maybe
i was counting on you
to hold me just a little tighter

love broke through
behind a lock that could not be picked,
my emotions weren't there to start.
'til you tore my walls down brick by brick
with your patience and gentle heart.

i had too many worries and doubts,
and a self-hate i could not expel.
but then you helped me turn it about
more than i ever helped myself.

i didn't know my heart could feel,
in fact, i thought i knew it couldn't.
you made my feelings something real,
i felt them when i knew i wouldn't.

though i didn't see the truth in time,
you were my light and i never knew.
until everything at last felt fine
and i could trace it back to you.

when finally your love broke through,
it was so clear for me to see.
but when in my heart i knew it true-

you were no longer here with me.

a piece of me
since your departure from my side
with a very essential piece of me,
i'm not so sure how i'll survive,
i can only say- *not easily*.

a measure of myself has left as well,
so i pray it's not too much to ask
what i now suppose only time will tell-

can a broken heart perform its task?

entry 14

you were like
a novel
a thriller i couldn't put down
until i unraveled the plot
the twists that kept me
enthralled and intrigued

it was that allure of a good book
of loving and savoring each page
until i realized
this is it
there is no plot twist

everything is as it seems
and i've wasted too much time
reading too many chapters

how did that binding
hold all those pages

with such a weak spine

entry 15

and loving you
was like waiting
for the beat to drop
after a desperately long buildup
that i needed
that my body ached for
to lead to something
tremendous

to vindicate my devotion
with something powerful
something i would feel
deep in my chest

but instead
here i am still
with this familiar
emptiness in my chest

because the bass never hit
and
we never did dance

never felt
for late nights spent with me in mind,
worried i don't have thoughts of you.
for wondering what you would find
if i could only tell the truth.

for random flowers left unsent
and casual kisses never given,
i know it's too late to repent
or to just now begin to listen.

and it won't take the pain away,
but for this and more, i blame myself.
for those three words you heard me say-

but now i know you never felt.

spoiled

i don't have a name for this type of regret,
but there's no way to misunderstand it.
hurting like this won't let you forget-

when you take a good heart for granted.

entry **16**

our spot was the playground
the one on the corner
we would only visit
late at night
because we both knew
we were too old for that
but we still had fun
laughing playing
like we were young

the swings the slide
and the lookout tower up top
that was my favorite

i guess for you
your favorite playtime thing
was always my heart

and i thought we both knew
we were too old for that

words from afar
what good are my words
devoid of a reassuring touch.
how can i remedy what hurts
when words are not enough.

and what is their effect
when spoken from far away.
it seems tangent to neglect,
with so much passion to convey.

how do i attempt
to keep you from afar.
i wish you'd never went,
so i could hold you where you are.

entry 17

why now
where was this
when i needed it

where were you
when my heart
begged
as i tried
to pry love
from your lips

when i invited love
deep into
every part
of my body
but got stood up
as you laid me down

when i searched
all of you
for its existence
night
after
night

as if that ever works

timidity
even when i at long last grasped
our love were there and it were true,
i failed to acknowledge it before it had passed-

and that's how i failed you.

entry 18

he sometimes
had this habit
of giving comments
rather than compliments

your hair
looks different
i've never seen
that dress before
and this or that
is interesting

descriptors devoid of
and detached from
sentiment

not often
would he allow
any emotion
in his words
to escape the shell
he'd built around his heart

only now i see
what a fragile shell it was

entry 19

i may not have
the answers
just yet

but finally
i'm starting
to figure out
what it is that
needs answering

at least i now know
those weren't shadows
dancing inside my heart

because when there is
no light left at all
it's just called
darkness

left alone
when your nights seem awfully long,
with time passing all too slowly,
we can meet and dance to our favorite song-

if alone ever feels too lonely.

entry 20

no
you don't get
to touch me
anymore
it was my voice
my words out loud
to him

but i was also
reminding myself
to not give in
to a touch

that same touch
i once pleaded with
to mean something

entry 21

love can be
all the difference
between caress
and grope

yet still

his most painful touch
is the one that
never was

may have been
the other day i thought of you,
it was a thought of you and me
that in my head i never knew
but my heart wanted to see.

a painting of what may have been,
from memories that were not made.
pretend stories from way back when,
a dreamt up world if you had stayed.

though we don't have that anymore,
no explanation, no because.
so now i'm left here longing for-

a time that never was.

entry 22

there were good things too
i can say that he was
handy and tidy
he would use
and return

the drill
back to the shelf
the hammer
back to the wall
the saw
back to the bench
my body
back to the smaller half of the bed

entry 23

though i admit it may just
feel that way now when
the flame is out when
there is no light
to guide my eyes
to tell my mind
what was real
to tell my heart
why it beats
or remind it
why it did

because
that's what is
important anyways
just how it feels and
how you did nothing to change that

entry 24

i used to be enough
for me

i used to radiate
my own light
and see plenty
in the world
to love

until i gave too much

i burned my light
too strong
for too long
lighting the way
for you

and now it's gone

all of you
you gave your all to me,
when i never did the same for you.
i'm gripped by thoughts of what i had and lost-

and to get it back, what i wouldn't do.

entry 25

there was only enough
love between us
to fill one

the more i gave
the more empty
i became

firsts

we speak of firsts as something treasured,
charms of a new beginning.
though where there's first, there's always final-

and those are much more stinging.

III

and yet, he did not know this girl before him.
or wait! he called out in excitement.
she glanced up and he was again confused,
those weren't the eyes that once adored him-
they were the eyes of one who'd been abused.
in that, he saw his own indictment.

no, he never laid a finger on her
and she knew he would not dare.
he was the one who couldn't be bothered
to let her know how much he cared.

he knew it inside but never did find
the place nor time to set it right in her mind,
just assumed she would be there tomorrow.
he waited 'til she was the one to decide-
there's always more time when the time
that you have is time that you have borrowed.

though even worse she had lent him the light
from right behind her eyes.
so that glimmer that he had chased for years,
it was nowhere again on this night.
it hadn't been there for some time he feared,
and as to why, he could well surmise.

faulty machine
if i could skip forward to the day
of whenever this hurt may end,
i would know time travel is just a myth-

if i'm not with her again.

entry 26

it was easy
to fall in love
with him

much less easy
to be in love
with him

entry 27

forgive but
don't forget
we often hear
though i need to
forgive and forget

to forgive myself
for having fallen for him

and forget
the things about him
that were worth falling for

singing alone
she didn't sing in the beginning,
she hardly spoke above a whisper.
but once her inhibitions thinned,
she started humming when i'm with her.

we'd drive for miles with nowhere in mind
and the radio turned on high.
to any song of any kind,
she'd sing along but barely try.

and if i dared turn the radio low,
she would switch to a gentle murmur.
she wasn't much for going solo,
it was clear she would not go further.

though once i heard her singing alone,
she had the voice of a living angel.
she didn't know i had just come home
and for that i was surely grateful.

i watched awhile then moved toward her
as she caught me in the mirror.
she was so amazing and i adored her,
but she would no longer let me hear her.

she hurried away, out of the room
and said *i never sing for anyone.*
i'm just too nervous, no matter for whom,
so i'm sorry, but now i'm done.

and i never heard her sweet voice again,
not like that time she was caught off guard.
i regret i couldn't put her at ease back then-

not enough to sing with all her heart.

hurt
it pains me so much
to know the hurt i put you through.
and just as bad is whatever hurt you had-

that i'm still oblivious to.

entry 28

some hurting you grow
so accustomed to
it's almost
soothing

a constant numb that
forbids any emotion
from taking hold
forbids you from even
knowing yourself
absent the pain

you can't love another
with this hurt inside
not really
you can't be happy
not truly

but at least
you can't get hurt again

entry 29

let me start
by loving me again
like when i was a girl

when i played outside and tucked
a yellow dandelion in my hair
and knew i was pretty
when my letters first formed words
and my numbers climbed past twenty
i knew i was smart
when i colored mostly inside the lines
mostly on the paper
i knew i was an artist
when my father kissed me on my head
and embraced all of me
i knew i was important

somehow my mind learned
to judge me by a set of ideals
that were not my own

who decided
that my dandelion was a weed

and why did i let them

would have stayed
i would have stayed 'til way past tired
to watch that last sunrise with you,
even built up a small fire
to keep us warm the whole night through.

i would have moved a little slower
through that last amusement park,
or maybe paid a little more
so we could stay there after dark.

i would have started one last season
of that show you really liked,
if it gave me one good reason
to stay up with you all night.

i would have ended our last walk
once the sky was slightly dimmer,
or got dessert to stay and talk
that last night we went to dinner.

stayed far later than intended
and driven home not quite as fast,
just to keep the night from ending-

if i had known it'd be our last.

back in time
if i could erase the harm i've caused-
go back in time and press record,
i'd change all of my flaws
and see all the signs that i ignored.

and i would fully be remiss,
yes, as selfish as it seems,
to have ever parted with
the very woman of my dreams.

i never wanted it this way-
i didn't hurt you by design,
but we hadn't met on that first day
with ever after on my mind.

so i'd go back to the beginning,
to where i first saw you on that night.
i would alter my misgivings
to be sure you're always treated right.

you'd say *hello* and i'd respond,
and probably with the same old grin.
i'd let it go a bit beyond
before i even changed a thing.

but soon i'd want to make you feel
that you're not in this thing alone.
maybe i'd cook your favorite meal
or invite you out over the phone.

and i bet you'd catch me staring
to see you happy once again.
i'd try to not be overbearing
or say things like *remember when?*

not to give myself away,
but i'd hold your hand a little faster.
do anything to stop that day,
the one we ended in disaster.

so there's a lot that i could do
if i were back in time with you.
though if i could truly start anew-

when you give your heart, i'd give mine too.

entry *30*

i don't speak to him
i won't
because i need
what's best for me now
and that's not him

i planned for this
practiced this
for various stretches
ahead of that last night
suppressing
distancing
avoiding
learning to breathe
without him

yet still i find
sometimes disregard
is almost as hard
as love

entry 31

i turn the radio on
and catch it
for a minute just at the end
of course it was
that song
that takes me back
to him to me and him
to back then

i turn the tv on
to a preview
for our favorite show
about a minute long
this season looks okay
of course it was
that show
from back then

i don't bother
with trying to read
because i know
i can't yet

turn the page

to a new chapter
in my book

someone
i never had faith in matching hearts
'til i found one to fit my own.
she was my most beautiful someone-

out of all the someones i've known.

entry 32

letting go can feel like
trying to hold
a funeral
for a
living
breathing
person

but if there's no heart beating
it's not so wrong and
it shouldn't be
so hard

enchanted memory
they don't behave much like memories,
not anymore, after all this time.
as surreal as simple reveries,
blurry daydreams of when she was mine.

the soft weight of her head on my chest
as her crazy hair tickles my nose.
kisses at dawn before we get dressed,
tracing shapes on my skin with her toes.

to think her lips once allowed that kiss,
her body sanctioned my hands to feel-
we're now so removed from all of this
that none of it today seems real.

fantasies that fill my mind just when
i fault myself and i ask aloud-

why did i not make her feel back then,
just as enchanting as she is now?

entry 33

it's as if i've
lost a journal
that i filled with
my most personal
thoughts and history and dreams
my most private self
on every page

and my journal is out there
somewhere

somewhere there's a stranger
who knows all that's in my mind

lucky
if i were bound to lose the one
who taught me love is true,
if that's as sure as the rising sun
in the east each day anew.

if i were destined to feel like this
and that's just the lot i drew,
if there had to be somebody i miss-

i'm still lucky because it was you.

there is no us, not anymore,
that's what i've now come to accept.
i picked myself up off the floor
and let go of the hope i've kept.

there's letting go and moving on,
i'd say i'm somewhere in between.
i hope someone can prove me wrong,
but there's none better that i've seen.

she gave me something that i feel
i may not ever find again.
and having known a love so real-

how could i ever play pretend?

entry 34

i envy those
who can draw
comfort from ink
but for me

not *breathe*
not *believe*
no *love*
no *hope*
no matter
what sage words
or which pretty font
there is no tattoo
i could fit on my wrist
that could possibly remedy
any of this

use sparingly
i haven't got much and yet i treasure it so-
a dash or a pinch, i haven't measured it though.
enough to get by today and last through the night,
if i add just a bit, i can make it alright.

i once had a whole lot- a few cups or a quart.
i would fill myself up just to still come up short.
all my wishes and wants, they would never end well-
such positive notions can be hard to expel.

when you're high on a hope that just cannot be met,
it's a far ways to fall and the heart won't forget.
so no passions, desires, no dreams, not a one-
i've now got a recipe for someone with none.

i'll use just enough hope to wake up tomorrow
and mark it as done so the next day may follow.
day in and day out, with such a certain routine-

too much hope in this life makes a bitter cuisine.

entry 35

most times
you can still see
faint marks of
the words that
once were important
and symbols that
once meant something
and sketches that
once told of dreams
someone had to erase

maybe not from afar
but if you ever get close

you'll see
stray lines of chalk
and often a dark spot or two
where someone wrote in marker
those stupid mistakes that
cannot be erased

i wonder if
there even is such a thing
as a clean slate

late of night
here it is, the pendulum's final chime
that beckons an endless spell from now 'til dawn-
a stretch unacquainted with father time,
when each moment herein is long and drawn.

here the clock is well known to be stubborn,
and each hour so unwilling to pass.
here laws of motion do scarcely govern,
and all sand stands still in the hour glass.

here the minute hand refuses to budge,
and every timepiece joins the resistance.
here passage of time won't give to a nudge,
and ages proceed, all in one instance.

here life moves, but not the seconds in queue,
and the dark may never find the day's light.
so moonlight reigns with no recess in view,
here in that most peculiar late of night.

entry 36

it's autumn now
not that pretty autumn
when the breadth of color
shames any painter's palette
but just beyond that

this is when
brown and dull
litter the land like
empty paper bags and
peanut shells after the circus

the liveliness the life
is over it means

but it's before
the winter comes
with a fresh coat of
white paint to pretend
death never visited here

this is the in between
that no one
can love

final night

do you suppose they know what doom, what fate?
though now veiled in esteem, with charm abound,
the aged blades will see soon what tomb awaits,
as grace fades, it seems, in haste on the ground.

these were no buds, not young- could they feel it?
of these new hues, does russet reveal it?
is their amber proud, perhaps defiant.
does crimson bear heat, rage of a giant.

do they look upon the pine with yearning?
learning somehow that in all honest truth,
their own purpose by design is churning,
turning anew to bring life from the root.

if so it must be a curious thing
that they've found calm in a furious wind,
bringing rest- yes, a final night for the blossom.
life is spring to autumn, this fight now exhausts them.

IV

still he steadied himself, and then he gave a grin
as if maybe he could prod it out somehow
if it were stuck somewhere deep within.
and he would be her champion
that brought it out to now.

he had waited so long for this moment here,
but could think not of a single question-
nothing to note from across the years
as she looked on with a polite expression.

that's the thing about a genuine smile-
a man must always earn it.
and here he was, it had been a while
and she could not return it.

now if you were to pass her on that path,
nothing troubles her, you might assume.
but you never knew her with that light
and so you'd never think to ask-
why the slightly different tune?
why the eyes that once lit up don't seem quite as bright?

nothing lasts
curiously, when filled, it requires much less tending,
as a full heart will float rather well on its own.
though now with such emptiness descending,
this hollow vessel will drop like a stone.

it's far heavier than one might assume,
what with it being merely just a void.
these abandoned chambers leave no room,
but for that of a fervent love destroyed.

so memories fade and with each, a bit of pain.
we learn to smile and read reaffirming quotes-
no, my heart's not broken. this was only a sprain,
and such thoughts of the quickest wits that ever wrote.

yet a vacancy remains within that sunken heart.
nothing lasts forever, more words meant to console.
it's true, painful memories do gradually depart,
until we're left with *nothing-*

which lasts forever i've been told.

entry 37

the world needs more of you
you once told me
in a teasing way

i blushed back then but
remembering now i think
maybe you were right

not in the way you meant it
but maybe that's exactly
what i need for myself

to look in the mirror
and be greeted with less
a reflection of what
someone else may desire
and in its place more of
who i am and who i want to be

i'm ready to be whole again
to be brimming with *more of me*

entry 38

there are a couple ways
for the soul
to retreat for a while

coffin and cocoon

but only one
leads to healing
and growth

flash flood
i finally feel distant from you, from us,
until i think of that laugh you'd make.
then playful memories rush my mind-

leaving feelings in their wake.

entry **39**

some time ago
i set out seeking
solace in my solitude
and serenity in my silence

a way to say
so long to this sadness

and i suppose i succeeded
since i've now started
to smile again

entry **40**

from every smile
affixed to a memory
but also every scar
that healed

from every highlight
and every flaw
in my story

a bit of who i am now
was woven into a
uniquely me fabric

and today
i think i like
this tapestry of me

things they say
we'll grow distant from each other,
from all the good times and the bad.
someday soon i'll rarely wonder
what became of the love we had.

what she's doing and whom with
since her and she was us and we,
and i won't mind who gets to kiss
her lips she once reserved for me.

these are all the things they say
with time are surely bound to happen,
yet based on how i feel today-

time must be stuck and barely passing.

entry **41**

perpetual motion machines
what fantastical things
are they

specifically
of a man's fantasy
that something may
just keep churning
for as long as he
wants it around

all with no energy in
maintenance kept
or effort given

i can't accept
any man who
expects me
to be that
something

a man who is
unaware or uncaring
that i will eventually

slow to a crawl
and burn out

not anymore

i vow to move for no man
who is not moving
for me

entry 42

i've learned to judge
my own worth
without him

but i keep searching
for a mold of him
in other men
like an old recipe
i almost got right
it was almost
what i craved

i haven't found it yet
but i think if i can
just attempt it
once again
with a fresh
batch of ingredients

only this time
i'll add just a bit more

loving me

coffee shop
today this one girl caught my eye-
she began to blush so i think she knew.
she kept my focus as i walked by,
so i smiled when she did too.

i was at the coffee shop alone
and she was by herself as well.
i had planned to sit down on my own,
but just then thought *what the hell...*

i said *hi* and we chatted awhile,
so i asked her to sit with me.
she agreed, still with that smile-
but she was much more than pretty.

the more we talked, i was left in awe,
she was brilliant and funny to boot.
simply exquisite from all that i saw-

the problem is she wasn't you.

entry 43

jigsaw puzzles
can be deceptive
some pieces seem
to fit together
just fine

and in our delight
we may not see
the small gaps
where none should be
or the slightly
mismatched visions
we're attempting to mesh

all the signs that
we're doing it wrong

entry 44

but i am not a rigid
cardboard piece with
a pre-painted picture

i can adapt
i can grow
i can be
as beautiful
as complex
as i choose
i am origami
both keen maker and
the delicate paper
the whole craft

with each crease
of every design
i shape my own story
create my own dreams
and celebrate those tales
on my own body and soul

i am woman and
i am art

like new
i have new sheets on my bed
that have never known your scent.
new dreams run through my head
without you guessing what they meant.

i have new clothes in my closet
and no idea if you'd approve.
a new phone in my pocket
and when it rings, it's never you.

i have new friends in this new town
and all new plans for what comes next.
still it can always knock me down-

to have to say that you're my ex.

dwindling wisdom
another year means one year wiser?
that's just not true from what i've found.
i'm not too certain i can keep that pace-

i think it's best if i count down.

find myself
i've been under the assumption
i needed her so i could feel,
as long ago i injured something
that with her gone, would never heal.

but i don't have her anymore
and i know that's for the better.
there's her request i had ignored-
just be yourself when we're together.

i was often scared to do this,
what would *myself* even have to show me?
but now i'm sure i must pursue him
before whoever else can know me.

to be that man i've never known,
i need to find out who *myself* is.
until then, i'm better off alone-

for my sake and whoever else's.

entry 45

this would have made you laugh
this little moment
from today

i wish i could put it out there
without you knowing
it's from me

and without you mistaking it for
a ticket for readmission
into my life

if only i could somehow pass it
anonymously through the ether
just for you

because it's not for everyone
maybe no one else would get it
but you

entry 46

when it's fresh
the things we
remember most
are the things that
hurt us most

the things that stab at us
nearly impale us
to encourage
corrective behavior

but as time passes
i find fond memories
cropping up
in unexpected places

a smile in my morning tea
a seduction in my wine glass

memories i can keep
that don't break me

how to clear a room
some say i'm proud, stubborn and callous,
as to why, i can only assume.
but look at me now, i've finally done it-

i'm the smartest guy in the room.

shatter
let it shatter, let it break,
run its course and see what happens.
take all the risks it wants to take
and let it crumble full of passion.

from one whose own was never open,
if there's some guidance i can give-

i'd say a heart that can't be broken
is a heart that hasn't lived.

entry 47

looking back did he not
hold me just as tight
regardless of whether
he knew it was love
fastening his embrace

did i not use
that embrace and
how tightly he held me
as a measure of
my own worth

i'm now stronger than i was
or rather i'm far stronger
than i ever knew

so can i blame him fully
for not knowing his heart
when i never knew my own
without him

best me
i couldn't grow without stormy weather,
i needed sunshine and the rain.
how could i expect to ever be better
without ever learning from pain.

that's what a man needs in order to change,
the sort of pain that he cannot control.
i've now known highs, lows, the whole damn range-
it's bad for the ego but good for the soul.

while i was the cause of all of this,
and far too often inconsiderate,
i have to evolve for my own happiness
for any change to be legitimate.

so now i'm sure i can finally say,
looking back, that i have grown.
i still make mistakes nearly every day-

but this is the best me that i've known.

V

if you're looking, you can find her-
she's as sweet and nice as ever.
she carries it well, her silent reminder,
she laughs and is just as clever.

but she now hums a song that's a little bit wrong,
though still, it's halfway decent.
with a heart that once beat for him so strong,
when in return it was only beaten.

and if he were now to ever endeavor
to bring back that light in her eye,
well, it's been said to never say never,
though it's not something riches can buy.

so he can give her all the world
and offer all the stars in sight,
yet it's barely just a start.
she's the girl
with a scar inside,
right across her heart.

entry 48

it's nearly spring now
as the snow recedes
and the battlefield
is fully revealed
for the first time

who makes it
through this far
who and what
survives the frost

the bare tree
still stands
the bear rises
from repose

but the flowers
were defeated
too delicate for conflict

and the monarchs
took flight
knowing they would be massacred

maybe
if each had been
just a bit stronger
they'd last

and maybe
what comes
once winter melts away
will come
with a new strength

but for now
the fragile things are gone

downtown

i saw her out downtown tonight
near the pub where we first met.
there she was by a dim streetlight,
as gorgeous as a girl can get.

it was late, the bars were closing
and she'd been dancing, it appeared.
i could tell by her dampened clothing,
and her makeup was slightly smeared.

but it didn't matter, not at all,
she was every bit as stunning.
it had been a while- no texts, no calls,
still my heartbeat started humming.

i couldn't say just how it felt
as i began to reminisce
on all the love that i once held
and all the memories i missed.

these thoughts and more just swarmed my head,
i did my best to shake them free.
to not think of all the words we've said,
or those we didn't and what it means.

but now all that's from bygone days
that seemed so distant 'til this night,
just when our eyes met in a gaze
and i thought *who knows what's right...*

i imagined i'd be stronger
if this time would come to pass,
that i would hold out a little longer,
but i walked her way across the grass.

on this very block where we had spent
such fun nights some time ago,
she took a step back from her friends
and offered a nervous *hello.*

i tried to think of something smooth
or witty that i could say.
but the truth is i could hardly move
or get my lips to reply with *hey.*

there was no ill will or any spite,
nothing too awkward i could sense.
just the two of us, late at night,
no expectations, no pretense.

and we talked about nothing crucial,
all in all it was fairly mundane,
but on the better side of neutral,
as if all our past were washed away.

it was then i found out i was wrong
about being better off alone,
all that nonsense about moving on
from the greatest girl i've ever known.

we didn't speak too long, in fact,
it was hard to get a read.
i couldn't guess how she'd react
if i attempted to proceed.

i kept cool, didn't cause a scene,
but really wanted her to stay.
for the first time say all that i mean,
with all the passion i could convey.

this time i thought better, though,
and figured it best to leave at that.
we said goodbye and i watched her go,
unsure if i might ever have her back.

but in that moment it was clear,
while contrary to all my claims,
there will always be a place right here-

with this girl, where my heart remains.

entry 49

how could i have known
such a brief embrace
would bring me
to a place
that feels
both foreign
and familiar

where
a familiar stranger
jumped my heart
and i realized
love can do that

so can ghosts

entry 50

forgive me
if i seem far away

my mind is lost
within a memory

and i may stay awhile

the way down
a snowflake's time is all so fleeting,
its very nature is ephemeral.
some quickly find the earth while speeding,
but i'd prefer the flight that's gentle.

from high up packed in a downy cloud,
i'd take a while and admire the view.
of all the crystals in a heaping crowd,
i'd float around 'til i found you.

would it not be nice to descend in tandem
with one fellow flake to enjoy the fall?
from down below it may all seem random,
but imagine there's enchantment to it all.

if given the choice, it's a feathery snow
where we dance and glide, with no sense of hurry.
a sheer breeze to guide us wherever we go,
in our romance begun of a light snow flurry.

we drift in a gust and skate on a current,
skimming thin air, catching light off of stars.
nothing else matters and nothing is urgent,
with you by my side anywhere that we are.

passing by mountains in a sweep together,
knowing we're soon to meet the ground-
it's truly a shame this won't be forever,
but let us rejoice since we have the way down.

what lies ahead
as time passes, i look back
on peaceful brooks and streams.
i know these pathways do not lack
hidden worlds and scenic dreams.

if i take that trail again someday,
i won't hesitate or worry.
i won't go through with it halfway
or be daunted by the journey.

i know what hides around these bends-
most the perils and the treasures.
if i ever had the chance again,
i'd be sure to do much better.

and i would be so glad
to be back this way at all.
if there are old complaints i had,
they're now so small i can't recall.

the forest views are so unreal,
though it's hardly an easy route.
there are some risks that made me feel
unsure at times or filled with doubt.

with all the thicket, the mud and hills,
what i would keep to get me through
is for all the storms and all the thrills,
the thought of walking next to you.

i may not know what lies ahead,
but i'd be ready for the task.
there's nowhere i'd want to be instead-

than right beside you on our path.

entry 51

he doesn't have to say it
not now when
his eyes betray him

after all this time
i finally know
his heart

i wonder as well
do my eyes betray me
and if so what do they reveal

my head would like to know
what my heart decides

entry 52

i still don't know
what comes next
but that's often when
you can look ahead
to each possibility
no matter how
unlikely or unlikable
it may have once seemed

it's all still possible
and that can be of comfort
when you have no idea what's next

entry 53

i don't believe you can lose
real love
not for good

time can be lost
sure
and in time you can
try to forget it
or lock it away
somewhere inside

you can probably keep it there
forever if you choose
but if ever you're ready
to wear it
on the outside again

that love
if it's real
it will be there

a letter
you'll meet a girl when you're unprepared-
she's full of life but somewhat fragile.
she'll give you all her heart laid bare,
your job is to be sure she can smile.

but please let her do the same for you
and i promise, she easily can.
now pay attention, there's often a clue
on how to be what she needs in a man.

she scrunches her nose if she's not mad yet
and you could turn this one around.
when she bites her lip, she's pretty upset,
but cheesecake may fix it, i've found.

sometimes she hits when she's delighted,
so you should look to earn a punch.
and when she gets real excited,
you just might receive a bunch.

if she's in bed, stuffed bunny in hand,
just know it's been an awful day.
so you should drop whatever you planned
and snuggle her pain away.

encourage her when she's burdened,
don't always try and fix what's wrong.
be there to listen, although i'm certain
she can handle most things on her own.

lend her your jacket whenever it's chilly,
then better yet, pull her in close.
do the small things that may seem silly-
what counts is the affection it shows.

now if she doubts even a bit
you think she's anything but perfect,
give her as much chocolate as you can get
until she knows she's worth it.

because she deserves nothing less,
i hope some of this may help.
so now you know how to love her best-

this letter's to you from your future self.

p.s. whenever you're given the chance,
     if she wants to dance- *dance*.

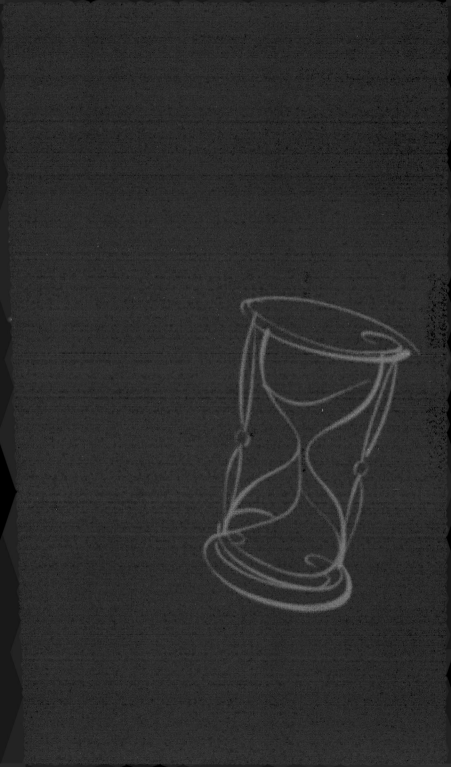

with a scar inside

if you're looking, you can find her-
she's as sweet and nice as ever.
she carries it well, her silent reminder,
she laughs and is just as clever.

though if one had known her before all this,
could they say she's just the same?
as if all those cardiac nicks and pricks
don't amount to lasting pain.

now time has a way of healing the damage
while leaving some bumps behind.
when sometimes it's more than a young girl can manage,
she finds herself slowly resigned.

so when he finally discovered
his heart was uncovered,
he said it proud but he said it too late.
when he told her at last he certainly loved her,
she could no longer relate.

yes, he sure took a while to show it,
but still he knew he loved her, yet.
he'll never see more gorgeous eyes
and now he's walked the miles to know it.

in his mind as bold, lined, italicized-
hers is a smile he'd never forget.

so you could say she's plain in style,
mild in demeanor.
some may pass her on the avenue
and swear they'd never seen her.
but for him- for one more chance to see that smile,
he took the only path he knew,
hoping that if he wandered for long
he would find her wandering too.

and over the years he traveled along
that same road quite a bit,
'til he heard an almost familiar song.
if he strained some- yes, it just might fit!
it's the same one she would often hum,
now just the notes were kind of altered-
the melody subdued.
twice he thought her pitch had faltered,
but his fingers nearly began to drum,
so it was close enough to true.

and yet, he did not know this girl before him.
or wait! he called out in excitement.

she glanced up and he was again confused,
those weren't the eyes that once adored him-
they were the eyes of one who'd been abused.
in that, he saw his own indictment.

no, he never laid a finger on her
and she knew he would not dare.
he was the one who couldn't be bothered
to let her know how much he cared.

he knew it inside but never did find
the place nor time to set it right in her mind,
just assumed she would be there tomorrow.
he waited 'til she was the one to decide-
there's always more time when the time
that you have is time that you have borrowed.

though even worse she had lent him the light
from right behind her eyes.
so that glimmer that he had chased for years,
it was nowhere again on this night.
it hadn't been there for some time he feared,
and as to why, he could well surmise.

still he steadied himself, and then he gave a grin

as if maybe he could prod it out somehow
if it were stuck somewhere deep within.
and he would be her champion
that brought it out to now.

he had waited so long for this moment here,
but could think not of a single question-
nothing to note from across the years
as she looked on with a polite expression.

that's the thing about a genuine smile-
a man must always earn it.
and here he was, it had been a while,
and she could not return it.

now if you were to pass her on that path,
nothing troubles her, you might assume.
but you never knew her with that light
and so you'd never think to ask-
why the slightly different tune?
why the eyes that once lit up don't seem quite as bright?

if you're looking, you can find her-
she's as sweet and nice as ever.
she carries it well, her silent reminder,

she laughs and is just as clever.

but she now hums a song that's a little bit wrong,
though still, it's halfway decent.
with a heart that once beat for him so strong,
when in return it was only beaten.

and if he were now to ever endeavor
to bring back that light in her eye,
well, it's been said to never say never,
though it's not something riches can buy.

so he can give her all the world
and offer all the stars in sight,
yet it's barely just a start.
she's the girl
with a scar inside,
right across her heart.

before we part

so that's all the story i can tell up to now. you know what i've done and what i never did- a lot of my faults and where i stumbled trying to walk my path blind. and you've seen what that did to someone i loved. i wasn't giving my all to her, because i didn't yet know my all- all that existed to give her.

self-knowledge can, in fact, should make for painful travel at times. i had attempted to bring another person on my path without knowing it nearly well enough myself and absent much effort to do so. that's a selfish thing, of course. and further along that road, there lay reality poised to knock me down. it turns out there was a lot of groundwork to do first. so that i'm still working on, along with a rough sketch map and stringing up some lanterns so i may walk that way with confidence one day.

so i hope you've now also seen my heart, you've seen my commitment to better myself, as this story has been my greenhorn journey in many regards. it's all the fruits of what discovering and traveling my path have given, some wonderful and some rotten. some, i've found, are wonderfully rotten with the proper perspective.

and i have learned a lot. i believe i'm now ready to share

that path with someone. you may be able to tell i've got someone in mind still, but i'm not sure if i'll ever again be trusted with the immense faith such a trek together requires. time will tell if i ever deserve another chance.

you may have noticed too, that time itself is a concept i return to often in my mind. i like to dream up ways it could be manipulated, what i might change, and what that would mean for my story. though we're of course only meant to experience time in a singular progressive fashion.

and somewhere on that timeline, we all get hurt, inevitably. that will happen. we can only hope most of that time is spent loving, and that though it may be deep, the hurting can go by as quick as a stolen kiss. going forward, that's my hope for all of us- and especially for the one i hurt.

but in the end, we'll just have to see how it all plays out, as time passes.

…i don't want
to not have you.

34623261R00088

Made in the USA
Middletown, DE
27 January 2019